Middle Aged and Kickin' It!

A Woman's Definitive Guide to Dating Over 40, 50 and Beyond

Gregg Michaelsen

Middle Aged and Kickin' It!
A Woman's Definitive Guide to Dating Over 40, 50 and Beyond

Gregg Michaelsen

Table of Contents

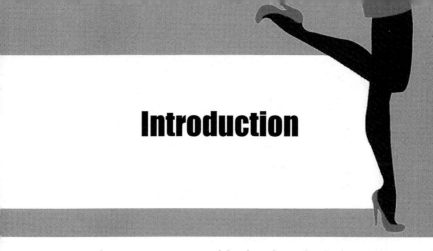

Introduction

Ladies, how amazing would it be if you had a no-B.S. guy's perspective on how to get back into the groove after a long hiatus from the dating world? You're reading this, so you have to be thinking now is the time. It's round two and you are pumped, you're ready to make a splash! It's time to get out there and find a good man, nay, an awesome man!

"Yes Gregg, that's exactly it! A fresh start is exactly what I need and I'm excited for round two! Well, except...I have no idea where to start, at all."

If you're over 40 and ready to start dating again, but don't know where or how to start, this is the book for you. If you want to find great man to share your life with—but also want to have some fun while you're finding him—then this book is your go-to.

Take It From a Guy Who Knows His Stuff

For those of you who don't know me, my name is Gregg Michaelsen and I'm an over-50 dating coach in Boston. I loved my past dating life and I still enjoy meeting new women. I love it so much that I became a dating coach, first for men, then shortly after, for women. It's something I **love** doing! I love helping men and women find great partners who make them happy - even after they think they've tried everything and have nowhere else to turn.

You've Taken a Huge Leap by Purchasing This Book

You're reading this now with a completely unique point of view on dating. Maybe you have kids or elderly parents whose care is your responsibility. Maybe you have a job that eats up all your time. Maybe you've been single for so long that you don't know where to start. Maybe you're recently divorced and your identity has been tied to someone for so long that you've forgotten who you were before.

No matter which road you've taken to get here, I can help get you back into the dating scene. That is a personal promise I'm making to you right now.

In this book:

- You will learn how to manage the baggage that comes with age and relationships

- You will understand what it takes to become **confident** again and feel amazing in your own body, no matter **what** you think you look like

- You will get fast tips on how to be relevant in today's dating world - not just how to look, but where to look

- You will learn how to have fun dating, and

how to make sure your next man treats you the way you want to be treated.

If all of that sounds awesome, then keep reading! This is the perfect book for you!

We all need a good shake up from time to time. Whether you're nervous about dating again, feeling guilty over obligations you have, or even complacent from being single for such a long time, I want you to shake it off, literally **shake it off** (go Taylor Swift on me), and say "I'm ready for a new start!"

Say this with me: "I'm beautiful, I'm ready for a fresh start, I'm EXCITED about dating again."

That's what I'm talking about!

Get your free info-graphic and learn *when is the RIGHT time to start dating again*.

Get it HERE:

http://www.whoholdsthecardsnow.com/middle-aged/

Chapter 1:
Suddenly
(Or Not-So-Suddenly)
Single Again

"Maybe you'll get married, maybe you won't. Maybe you'll have children. Maybe you won't. Maybe you'll divorce at 40, maybe you'll dance the funky chicken on your 75th wedding anniversary."
–Mary Schmich

I may be the one writing this book, but **you** are the one with a story to tell. Nobody over the age of 40 who jumps back into the dating world can say they're free of drama and baggage. I get it, trust me! My story reads more like a Stephen King novel than it does a Disney musical. Maybe you think your own story shares a similar trend. I'm here to tell you you aren't alone, not by a long shot.

We can't banish those tough life experiences, and in most cases, why would we want to? Those experiences are our lives. In some cases, that difficult first marriage resulted in the children you love so much. Perhaps you're widowed and simply cannot imagine replacing the husband you still love today. While these experiences have colored your life, they may also be holding you back from dating. They may be chipping away at your confidence even now, making you think you're "un-dateable."

I'm here to tell you no matter what baggage you're bringing to the table, you are a **catch** and men out there **want** to date you! I'm serious! The single most important takeaway from this chapter is that **you are dateable**. No matter what you've been through, no matter what your ex-husband, ex-lover, ex-whatever said about you, you are 100% **unique hot stuff!**

This Ain't No Fairytale

Life isn't a Disney movie. We aren't living in a Nicholas Sparks novel. God is not a romantic comedy writer scripting you as the protagonist in his next big blockbuster hit. You're simply you, complete with baggage, a job, kids and more ex-lovers than you'd care to relate to mom.

Furthermore, all those "perfect marriages" that you know in real life *aren't perfect*. They're flawed, difficult, and frustrating. The only difference between your life and theirs is that they close their windows and doors before they start yelling at each other. They air out their dirty laundry in the backyard behind 6-foot walls. They probably fell into love just as you may have. They didn't test the waters for long and they spent more time as someone's "better half" than they did as their own "complete whole."

In order to find an awesome guy, you'll need to feel comfortable being **without** one. I recommend this to all women, not just the ones who have recently left a long-term relationship. If you don't take the time to understand your own value, you'll never be successful in the dating world, let alone the relationship world. Confidence is everything, and this chapter will provide the seeds to make that confidence possible.

What is Your Worst Fear ~~Fear~~   Fears.
When It Comes to Dating at This Age?

Go ahead, answer the question above. It's going to be the first thing that comes to mind. It's also going to be your **biggest** excuse for staying away from dating. Why? Because this is where you also fear being rejected the most. This is where you feel rejection would hurt the most.

Take a look at the list below. These are the most common excuses I hear as a dating coach. Chances are if you're nervous about jumping into the dating world again, one of these issues is the culprit.

(1) **I'm not as pretty as I was in my 20's.** I've put on weight. I haven't gone to the gym in years. No guy in their right mind would find me attractive. I have wrinkles...men hate wrinkles!

(2) **There aren't any good guys left to date at my age.** That's right, all the good ones are taken. They got married years ago and are in great relationships living in suburbs in houses with white picket fences.

They've got beautiful children who go to private schools 5 minutes away from where they live. Anyone I'd meet now is bottom-of-the-barrel material... oh God am I bottom-of-the-barrel material?!

 I'm a package deal who comes with kids, cats, and dogs. I've got a train of other people and animals following me around. I would feel guilty if I brought someone else into the house. How can I spend money and time on dating when I have kids to think of? And even if a guy accepts me, how will he accept everyone else who comes *with* me? Don't guys hate responsibility anyway?

 No guy wants to deal with a divorcee. If I tell him I'm divorced, he'll wonder if I'm some kind of train wreck waiting to happen. Plus, my ex is still around, either paying child support or picking up the kids on weekends. How weird would it be if they met each other?

 I'm up to my ears with work, and guys want more attention from me than I can give. I'm really hitting my stride at the office and now might not be the best time to start dating. I'm lonely but I guess that's the way it has to be.

Any of this sound familiar? If it does, then *don't worry*. In Chapter 2 I'll show you how you can turn every one of these fears into **benefits.** No joke - the fears you have inside of you making you certain that you're un-dateable are the very things a guy may find attractive about you. You just don't realize it yet!

The Basis of Confidence: Clean Laundry

This chapter is your first step toward having the confidence you need to make a big splash in the dating world. Best of all, this first step has one very simple requirement-time.

Take a look at this diagram:

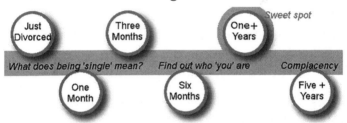

There is an *ideal* time frame for jumping back into the dating world. Too soon after a divorce or break up (from a very committed relationship) and you'll be making poor decisions based solely off your emotions rather than reason, which is **never** a good scenario. But, if you wait too long, you risk becoming complacent in your singleness, and may even stay single the rest of your life.

feeling confident in yourself
no need to change

Let's imagine you're sitting somewhere between "Just Divorced" and Three Months. This time frame is emotionally exhausting and could require moving, breaking up assets and a whole slew of other issues. At the same time, you're readjusting to being single—maybe after a decade or more of being with someone. You may **feel** happy—even ecstatic—but you are **not** okay. This is a time for healing, not hunting down your next long-term partner.

I don't think many women reading this book are in this time frame, but if you are, I'd highly suggest spending time with your friends and family, especially your children. Do things which make you happy and avoid the dating scene for the moment (you've got plenty of time for it in the near future!)

What happens when you move into the area of Six Months to a Year? As we get into Chapter 2, you'll hear me talk about getting to the *real* you, the one who may have been covered up for the past few years. During this time frame, you may want to try some things that make *you* happy. Don't feel pressured to look for someone else. If you want to date, you can, but *do not commit*. It is still too soon and any attempts at committing to a relationship at this point will likely fall apart. This is time for *you*, and that means doing what makes you happy and spending time with the people who are important to you.

Once you've reached the One Year mark, make a concerted effort to start dating again. Ideally, you won't absolutely despise your old ex anymore. If you still loathe him uncontrollably than it's a sign you still need time to heal. Some wounds take longer to heal than others. The more you talk to friends and family about this, the sooner you'll be ready to get into a committed relationship again.

If you've been single for Three+ Years, you may be complacent. I've got a test for this. If you open up your freezer and all you see are Hungry Man dinners, the only produce you have in your fridge is limes for shooting tequila, and the last thong you owned was thrown away back in '89, then you're probably over-complacent. You may think you're just too busy doing your thing to start dating again.

If you're in this category and you picked up this book...awesome news for you! You're willing to give the world of dating another try. You just need a helping hand to get started again.

Getting Right with Yourself

Airing out your dirty laundry takes time. If your emotions are running high from a recent divorce, your time is best spent healing and enjoying the comfort of friends and family—not looking for another commitment. Similarly, if you wait *too* long, you can become complacent, and feel *so* comfortable being single that you may one day lose all interest in having a committed relationship.

In the end, everyone heals differently. It's up to you to know how long you need to get over your last relationship.

Healing and Moving On

I already mentioned the primary ingredient for moving on after an extensive relationship - time. Without time in between you and your last committed relationship, you'll base all dating decisions off of raw emotion.

Of course it's important for emotions play *some* part in your dating life. How could they not? However, if their role is *too* large, you will make terrible dating decisions. By that, I mean you will fall in love with a scumbag player who uses you for sex and then dumps you...or some crazy Nigerian dude who claims he's a Frenchman, sends you love notes via email, and then asks you for money for a plane ticket, *only to never show up.* Trust me ladies, **this kind of crap happens all the time when you let your emotions govern *every* action you take.** Taking the time to get back to neutral territory is a MUST.

One of my favorite dating books for women, *The Power of the Pussy*, talks about this kind of raw emotion in detail:

> *"Allowing our emotions to influence our actions and decisions is what gets us into trouble,"* says Kara King, author of the book. *"It serves no purpose whatsoever. It may give short-term satisfaction, but it always leads to greater heartache."*

Time + Diversion = The Basis for Great Dating

Now we know the most important part of the equa-tion - time. The _second_ most important part is _diver-sion._ Before you jump back into the world of dating, before you can get right with the world, you need to pursue activities _other than dating_ which will help keep your brain entertained. **If you're watching The Notebook with a gallon of ice cream in your lap you are not doing it right.** That's not diversion. That's emotional gluttony. And it's making you feel worse, not better.

In Chapter 2 we'll talk about ideas for breaking out of your depression and making a _real_ life for yourself and I don't mean a life full of work and chil-dren. These things are very important to your iden-tity and they're helpful diversions to some extent, but we want to take it a step further. We want to create both _diversion_ and _personal value_ at the same time. These two things are **essential** if you want to find an amazing guy!

Addressing the Guilt

Ladies, before you begin to date again, you need to address your own guilt. I cannot count the amount of times I've heard these statements as a dating coach:

- "Gregg, I've tried going out on dates, but I spend a lot of money making myself look great then I feel guilty that I'm not spending that money on the people who are already in my life, like my kids."

- "Gregg, if I'm out even once a week on a date, I need to find a sitter for my kids and they wonder where I am. I feel bad, I almost feel like I'm putting them second."

- "Gregg, what if I bring someone back to the house when my kids are home? My kids are still young and love their father. How can I make space for a new guy? How can I convince my kids this new guy isn't a threat?"

What's the one common thread on all of those above quotes? Kids - and boy do they make it hard for women to get back into the dating scene!

The amount of guilt women truck around when it comes to their children is understandable. They were there before any new guy came around, so it stands to reason that they should come first. Women also have no desire to traumatize their children by bringing home random guys on the weekend. Loud sex with a new partner when the kids are home? Uh, no thanks.

As a parent, you're inclined to shield your children from anything which could cause them stress, frustration or confusion. Dating someone else who isn't 'Dad' can increase the likelihood of all three. So let's talk about how we can mitigate some of these issues. There are easy solutions which will dramatically reduce any issues your children have with you dating.

Tip #1: Talk to your kids!

Yes, really talk to them about you dating again, as if they were grown up human beings who have a say in whether you start dating or not. Ask for their opinion. Tell them how you feel. I know you want to shelter your children, but by not talking to them, you're creating confusion, misunderstanding and resentment. The longer these fester, the more likely it is you'll give up dating altogether.

They need to know the reasons *why* you're dating. Ask your kids how they feel about it, and answer questions which come up about dad. These are *not* easy questions but you need to start the conversation, ideally **before** you start dating again. If your children give you their blessing to start dating, it is a **huge** weight off of your shoulders.

This is the single most important tip I have. They may not like it at first. They may scream their heads off and twist your words. Don't give up, tell them how you really feel, and they *will* eventually be okay with the idea of you seeing other guys.

Tip #2: You'll feel less guilty once some time has passed

Ugh, Gregg, again with the time? But honestly, if you are lonely and you start bringing men home a month or two after the big divorce, you're doing it all wrong! Of course your kids will freak out. They'll think you don't care about them, and you *never* cared about dad. Time will allow your children a bit of breathing room to get used to the separation. This could take *months,* but if you date too soon, the relationships won't go anywhere anyway.

Tip #3: Don't force your kids into a meeting with the new guy
This applies especially to teenagers. Let some time pass, give your kids some space, and never force them to go out with you and Bob. It won't happen overnight but if you're patient, it will eventually, then you won't feel insanely guilty every time you beg your kids to hang out.

Tip #4: Set up a date night schedule and stick with it
Set expectations early, and stick to them. Have a set dating schedule which you religiously follow. Start small at first, and make sure it's on a night where not much is going on with you and the kids. Even better, on a night where your ex has them. Don't forget to talk to your kids about this night. *Tell them why it's important to you.*

This isn't just about dating though - you'll also be on dating sites, ignoring your kids. You'll be talking to some new guy on the phone, ignoring your kids. You'll be thinking of how cute this guy you just met is, and ignoring your kids. When you start dating, this stuff just *happens*. You get into it! That's a great thing, but it also needs to be tempered. Wait until everyone is in bed and have an hour just for 'you'. You can chat away with someone, rework your online profile and daydream until your heart's content.

When those boundaries fall apart (and they will from time to time) I have one last piece of advice...

Tip #5: Acknowledge to your children how insane this whole situation is making you

Be honest! If you've jumped into the dating world again, you're probably terrified, excited, happy, depressed and jittery—sometimes all at once! You don't need to relate every new guy who comes into your life to your kids. But *tell* your kids you're sorry in advance, and they will appreciate your honesty and more importantly, *cut you some slack.*

Of course, kids aren't the only source of guilt. Women in their fifties and sixties might be dealing with caring for their elderly folks. This is time con-suming and can be emotionally draining. I know, I'm 53, and I too am dealing with my folks. When you are driving home after visiting your Mom in the nursing home or hospital, the last thing you want to think about is your own life. It makes you feel selfish.

And yet, we must! Life does not stop because bad things are happening around us. Bad things are always happening around us. I'm here to tell you to compartmentalize your life at times. Some part of every hour, day or week needs to be set aside for you, *fun* for you with **no** guilt! It's tough, I know, but you must change this course or, before you know it, you will be the one in the nursing home wishing you stopped and smelled the roses!

The Foundation for Real Confidence is in Your Hands

Chapter 1 is an important first step for any woman who considers jumping back into the dating scene after a long break. Let's go over the highlights of what we just learned:

- You are not the only person over 40 looking for a fresh start with a fresh relationship. I'm just one dating coach and I've spoken with dozens of women who need advice on how to get started again. Many of them have found amazing partners, and others are enjoying the dating scene so much, they haven't wanted to leave it quite yet!

- You're coming to the table with more baggage than you had in your 20's. That's totally fine and completely normal. In later chapters, I'll explain how to manage baggage on dates. In Chapter 2, I'll explain why baggage isn't as bad as you think it is (and may even be considered attractive by someone who shares the same experiences as you do.) The most important thing about baggage is to *accept it and feel comfortable about it.* This takes *time,* especially after getting out of a long-term committed relationship.

- Consider how much time has passed since your last relationship. Is it too early to start dating? Are you complacent being single?

- Time is just one factor when it comes to getting over a relationship. Having fun and diverting your attention away from all of the emotion you're carrying around with you is critical.

- There are ways to manage the guilt you feel about dating. Take the time to talk to your kids and make sure when you *do* start dating, you start dating the right way.

- Some part of every hour, day or week needs time put away for you, ***fun*** put aside for you without any guilt! *Compartmentalise*

It's time to move onto Chapter 2. Get ready to learn all about feeling confident again. And trust me: without a doubt, confidence is the single most important thing you'll bring to the dating world.

Chapter 2:
Finding the Confidence
to Date Again

Why Confidence Matters

Here's a question for you: what transcends looks, money, fame, personality and anything else we consider to be important when we're on the lookout for a great partner?

The answer, of course, is confidence. Plain and simple, confidence is the greatest asset you can have in the dating world. Period.

Before we begin this chapter I want you to watch this powerful video:

You are more beautiful than you think
https://www.youtube.com/watch?v=XpaOjMXyJGk

I can cry every time I watch this. It is that powerful and true. This video (by Dove) hits at the very core of what I teach in all my books.

Play it again.

I'm not joking, I'm not playing any trick on you. I'm being dead serious. You come to the dating scene with confidence oozing out of your pores and you will be irresistible to men!

Confidence is powerful enough to make women

and men date people uglier, poorer, less interesting and less emotionally stable than they are. Simply put, human beings, men *and* women, feed off of the confidence exuded by others. It makes them feel better about themselves and their actions. It makes them feel wanted, desired and respected.

Confidence is important for any human interaction, but we want to keep this on topic as it relates to the dating game. Let's take a look at a few reasons why growing your own confidence will not only enhance your dating life, but the relationships which come *out* of your dating life.

Confidence helps you manage rejection

Rejection happens ladies, and it's going to happen to you once you jump back into dating. Accept it right here and now: you're *going* to get shot down! I'm a dating coach and even I get shot down. You'll be shooting guys down too if you're doing it right.

Everyone on the face of the planet has been rejected by *someone* while they've been dating, excluding some weird exceptions like arranged marriages and other anomalies. I'm not saying it's painless because it does hurt. It *will* hurt, but confidence helps you pick up the pieces and move on to another guy *faster.* Why? **Because you know you're valuable!** So what if some guy isn't interested in taking you out on a second date? You know you're awesome. Who cares what he thinks anyway?

Without confidence, however, you'll be hung up on those rejections - Every. Single. Time. You will be sitting there wondering what you did wrong, what you should do to change yourself, whether it was your hair, something you said or something you did. The list goes on and on! If this is your attitude you will never make it in the dating world!

Confidence helps you make better choices in men
Women who aren't confident fall for men who aren't awesome. It's as simple as that. You don't see why anyone would enjoy your company or love you for you, and therefore you pick the lowest of the low. You sniff around the bottom of the barrel because that's where the guys who would accept you for who you are hiding.

Excuse my French – **Bullshit**! If you're reading this, you're valuable. You're unique, you're one-of-a-kind and with a helpful push from confidence you could date guys that treat you with respect and love you for who you are.

Will confidence help you get any man you want? No, it won't, and you'll still get rejected. That's fine! Your goal is to find a great man who accepts you for you. **Confidence helps the real value in you shine out like a beacon for the rest of the world to see.** Not all guys will find certain values important. Maybe you're an amazingly caring mother and nurturer. While this may make you incredibly valuable to one man, it won't make you interesting to some start-up tech exec looking for a career-driven CEO who owns her own company and drives a Beemer. That's **okay**! You'll find a guy who loves you for you. It just takes time, and lots of confidence in yourself.

Confidence pushes you to make better life decisions

A confident woman will be a decision maker in her own life. She won't let a man dictate what she can and cannot do. She finds enjoyment outside of men *and that in turn makes her more attractive to men.*

You may find confidence in a job, in a hobby, in caring for friends and family or in volunteer work. What is important is for you to identify what it is that gives your life value and then learn more about it and experience it to actually *see* it as valuable. This helps you feel in control of your own life. **You** are the one dictating what's important for you. When you find a man who is worthy of that value, you may consider keeping him around. Until then, guys can come and go, since you generate your value elsewhere.

Confidence keeps relationships going longer

Women feel the need to care for their men, and in doing so they tend to give up things they shouldn't. This might be friends, a favorite hobby and even a promotion at work. This may seem wise at the time, but it only undermines the thing that attracts him to you the most: your value.

Once you're only there to support *him*, the value erodes and so does your confidence. You become

unsure of yourself because every time he disap-
proves, you worry. You fear losing him more than
ever, which in turn makes him even more repulsed
by you. This happens to thousands and thousands
of relationships. If you want to find a committed life
partner, you cannot lose your value. Once self-value
disappears, so does confidence and the relationship
will follow.

By all means, compromise with him, but don't
give in to him. If you're hanging out with your
friends and he calls, don't run to him. He'll respect
that and love you more because of it. As you'll see
in the coming chapters, this kind of action attracts
men like nothing else!

Finding What Makes You Valuable

Remember the list of worst fears that I talked about
in Chapter 1? Well, let's go over a few of them again,
only this time, we'll talk about how each one can be
perceived as a **benefit** to the right man.

I'm not as pretty as I was in my 20's. Who said all
guys are looking for women who look like they're
in their 20's? While you're worried about your age
and a few added wrinkles (if you even have any)
guys are out there **begging** to have a woman like
you in their lives. Men ten years your senior would
feel 10 years younger *just by being around you.* The
more you embrace your age and the sex appeal that
comes with it, instead of demeaning yourself and

feeling old and ugly, the better you'll look and feel.

Don't think for a second it's only older men who dig women your age. Younger men *love* older women! You don't believe me? All right, here's a source that (sadly) men trust: PornHub. According to PornHub, MILF porn is the third most popular search category on their website! (Ah, forgive me if you weren't aware of what that acronym means: Mom I'd Like to Fuck.) There you have it!

Would you believe "mom" is the most common term used in search engines on PornHub? Huh, that's interesting. What's the deal with all these guys pining over older women with kids? Weird, right? Maybe to you, but not to the millions of single (and not-so-single) men out there! To them, you're a hot commodity!

Embrace your age. I'm telling you, **embrace your age!** If you're a confident woman over the age of 40, you *are* sexy and men want to have you! Get to a mirror, look your hot self in the eyes, and say **"I'm hot and men would kill to date me!"**

I'm a package deal who comes with kids, cats, and dogs. I bet you care a great deal for your children and your animals. I bet you'd do anything for them and love them more than you ever imagined you'd love anything. Ladies, these things give you *value*. Let me reiterate: women of value are **hot stuff**.

That's not even the best part. The best part is you can already make a connection with a man who shares similar values with you. Yes ladies, there are men out there who share the same love for their children and animals as you do. That's an instant bond right there. You both have a similar passion and that's an amazing thing to share!

I'm up to my ears with work, and guys want more attention from me than I can give. Men love women who are too busy for them. Really! Again, it has everything to do with a woman's value. If she's working and can't drop everything just to go on a date with some guy, then that shows she has other priorities outside of him.

Plus, a woman who is holding down a job and bringing in her own income is attractive to many men. In this case, they want an empowered woman who makes her own money, not a woman who is at home all day doing chores or running errands.

And, by the way, if you can find time to read this book, you can find time to go on a 90-minute date once a week! Work definitely keeps us busy but it doesn't have to take up *all* of our time. Growing your connection with a great guy is a very worthwhile pursuit, and one who may be worth cutting your work back from 12 to 10 hours a day.

No guy wants a divorcee. If you're a beautiful, confident woman, it doesn't matter if you've been married before or not. We'll go over how to handle your ex in a future chapter but for now, know that a good guy will ignore that fact entirely if he finds you to be an amazing person. Heck, he may find you *more* attractive because you share similar experiences. It doesn't matter _why you were_ divorced. What matters is that you're both *been there.* You've been in one another's shoes and can relate.

Behind Enemy Lines:
How to Find Confidence and KEEP IT.

Let's imagine you are your own worst enemy, and that enemy territory is the mantra you tell yourself over and over: "I'm going to lose weight," I'm going to advance my career," I'm going to stop giving in to guys and start thinking of my own needs."

Sound familiar? Well in this segment, I'll help you break bad habits and replace them with positive ones.

Bad habits have probably built up over *years*. It happens. The problem is many of these habits are self-destructive and you'll want to address them before you jump into the dating world.

Here's the general idea. You know how to train your dog to give you his paw, right? Grab his paw and give him a treat. If he raises it half way, praise him, then pull his paw up into your hand again. No paw? Discourage him by changing your voice and withholding the treat. When he does it on his own you say, "Good doggie" in a happy voice and reward him with another treat.

Rinse and repeat.

Easy! Dogs do it all the time and they're not nearly as smart as we are. And yet most of us can't reprogram squat in our lives. Why is that? Well, we're scared for one. Making changes could bring us failure, and we can't stand that. So we stay in our own little ruts for years, making excuses about why we never break the cycle.

We get sick of this lifestyle for sure! There are times we get angry and we act. The problem is we try to find the easiest way out. Take smoking for instance. People will try hypnosis, the Patch and New Year's resolutions, but this is just a list that gets us nowhere. We fail and are back at square one.

Ninety-two percent of us say we have screwed up at least one New Year's resolution. You'd be crazy to think you're any different.

The right way, unfortunately, is often the hard way. I've had to train myself on more than one occasion and trust me, the **one** thing I can guarantee is that starting **right now** is the only way that it can be done. No "I'll start on Monday" B.S., no "New Year's resolution" crap. Right now is the only way, and it will require plenty of action to make it stick.

We can't put off meaningful change and expect our lives to be any different than they are today. When I coach women, I know the ones who will change—almost immediately. The ones who will change will be the ones who want change to happen *immediately* so they can start **now**. The others? They're wasting their time and money with me.

My Experience with the Right Now Mentality

Five years ago I was fat. I was so fat, I couldn't see my own penis over my gut...yes it was that bad. But hey, I didn't care! My girlfriend loved me and I love yodels and chocolate chips so all was good. She even bought me yodels (maybe she was trying to keep me fat, or she thought I was Santa - I don't know) so I continued my quest to be a hippo. We went to Aruba and, upon returning, I saw myself in pictures with my beautiful girlfriend. OMG! It just didn't dawn on me until that moment how much I had let myself go.

That night, I looked for a solution. It wasn't a matter of *if* I was going to lose weight; it was a matter of _how I was going to do it and what the_ **most** effective (**not** the easiest) way to lose weight would be. In fact, I was so committed, angry, you name it, I wanted to take it a step further – I wanted to be ripped!

I bought P90X and I crushed it. I cried, I screamed, but I did it and I found my penis again! After 90 days, I repeated it with P90x+, and then Insanity. Today I am still doing the workouts.

My point is this: It's very simple. If you want change, if you want to break your routine and train yourself you need *four* things:

- **Massive** Action

- It must happen **now**, not tomorrow and not after the New Year

- Repetition - just like a dog, you must **repeat it over and over** until a new habit forms

- **Praise** yourself during the process

Notice I didn't mention a shrink, Doctor Phil or a witch doctor with her sharp pins and doll who looks like you.

You Are NOT Above the Process

Those four steps aren't just good ideas, they are requirements. Unless you get motivated to act **now**, it's very likely that you will never act. You might mean well. You might say you'll get started as soon as this or that happens. But until you act you're just part of that 92% number I mentioned earlier.

Remember - massive action, right **now**, followed by repetition and praise. It's funny, but praise can often be the part we forget, and yet it's essential to the process! Just like the pup we mentioned earlier, you need to give yourself a pat on the back and a treat (or some new shoes!) to ensure you keep following through. For instance, when I completed my first 30 days of P90X, I treated myself to an hour massage at a salon downtown.

You don't need huge rewards to make change happen. The motivation of seeing results is enough! I lost 5 pounds and I could see my penis again. That was reward enough for me!

Gregg, What happens If I Fail?

If you fail, let it **only** be for one day, and then work even harder the next. If you stop for good, you have given your brain an excuse to give up – **don't**. Don't beat yourself up either. Just forget about yesterday and do it **better** today. Your mind and body will be happy. Repeat this until you are over the hump, then your brain won't try to sabotage your goal anymore because your goal will be your new routine.

They say it takes 21 days to form a habit. Make the first 21 days count and then see where you are!

I love McDonalds. I would be hungry, head over for a burger and then feel terrible. I stopped thinking that way and addressed the situation by never driving by a McDonalds when I was hungry (basically eating before I set out) and this problem was not an issue anymore.

The beauty of my formula is that you can plug anything you want into it and become obsessed, like I do, by getting outstanding results. I find it easy now to break a habit and form another.

I am making smoothies now. My blender has been sitting in my closet for three years. I hate peeling, buying, and eating fruit but I knew I could like smoothies. I said, "I need smoothies!" I googled an easy recipe with tons of reviews, went to the store and got fruit (I had to ask what a mango looked like) and I raced home, peeled the stinkin' mango, tossed in the banana, 5 strawberries, a cup of blueberries, ice and **snap**...I had made my first healthy smoothie. I was so proud of myself!

Next day – more smoothies.

Final tip, I promise! When you are training yourself, look for your weaknesses and attack them. Most people do the opposite. If you concentrate on what you are not good at, the easy stuff will be your reward. If you suck at engaging a guy in a conversation, then do that first! You will realize that your mind made it a much bigger deal than it really is. Make a plan around the tough stuff. Meet your girlfriends later in the night, and in the meantime you can work on the cute guys at the charity event while you wait for them.

Throughout the rest of this chapter, I want you to remember this framework. Later on, you'll come up with a goal **you** want and you're going to get to work!

Overcoming the "Un-Dateable" Mentality

When you first consider dating again, you'll try to come up with reasons why you shouldn't. These are meant to keep you safe, to avoid rejection and maintain the status quo.

You deserve more than this. All of the reasons you're thinking of right now are bull: I'm too old, I've been out of the dating game too long, I've got too much baggage—all of it needs to be dumped out the window right now. You're an attractive woman who wants to find a man who complements her and will grow a life with her. A man who makes her happy.

So where do we start? Well, I'll tell you right now, *it doesn't start with just blindly going out there and dating away!* This might be true of a woman whose self-confidence is already soaring through the roof. If that's the case, by all means, get out there and date!

But for women who are either suddenly single or complacently single, it's a different matter entirely. We need to set the stage for confidence first because as you remember, without confidence, you can't guarantee you'll get a **good** guy. And that's what we're looking for right? Not just another crummy relationship, but the **real deal**. A great man!

Going Social

You may be terrified of that first date. Or perhaps you have started dating again but you feel completely out of your element. In either case, I believe the problem is the same - you're reaching for the moonshine when you should be pouring yourself a wine cooler. You need to ease into the dating world, not cannonball into it!

Let me ask you a question: on a scale of 1 to 10, where 1 is non-existent and 10 is awesome, where is your social life now? Think about when the last time was you went out for drinks with friends, out to a restaurant, or even to a bar with some co-workers for happy hour. Is it every week, once a month? Do you even remember the last time you did something like that?

Depending on where you are on that scale, you may need to consider a complete social-life overhaul.

"But Gregg," I can hear you asking right now, "why does that even matter? I'm about to start dating again, isn't that a social life?"

No. No it is **not**. You should consider dating as part of a **broader** social life. Why? Again, it comes down to value. A woman who has a social life outside of a man *is going to land a better man*. It makes her more confident. It shows her that she can be pickier when it comes to choosing men because now she's looking for men who are equally engaged in their own social circles.

This is the equation you need to follow:

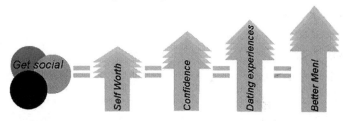

If you BEGIN dating with an active social life, **everything** else will fall into place.

The First Steps to Achieving an Active Social Life

First thing's first, there are two requirements for a total social life makeover: **time** and **a desire to better yourself**. If you have both, then you can get started **today**.

If you rated yourself a 7 or higher on that 1 to 10 social life scale which I mentioned earlier, then you can skip this section of the book. I wrote this to give women with little to no social life a serious boost in both confidence AND ideas.

And ladies, let's be serious here. If you're not confident about your social life, how confident will you feel in your dating life? Pretty easy question to answer, right? So get out there first, have some fun, get to know other *single* women who are enjoying themselves, and *then* meet some guys.

Did I throw you a curve ball with the *single* women part? Here's the hard truth - your married friends are going to bring you down. They're going to give you advice and ideas when the truth is **they don't know what they're talking about!**

Again, *don't take advice from your married friends.* They're in their own little bubble worlds, just like you were when you weren't dating and going out. They mean well, but that doesn't cut it anymore. You need new friends who are in your shoes and under-stand what you're going through; friends who will flood your head with cool ideas and things to do.

Lastly, when you start dating again, you'll have people who you can talk to *who aren't critical about your dating decisions!* They'll give it to you straight because they understand what you're going through. A married woman isn't going to do that! They're already critical of your situation and their advice will only bring you down.

You know *who* you're looking for (single women around your age) - now, where do you find them?

"Gregg, do I have the wrong book?" I started off looking for single men, now I'm looking for single *women?* You aren't doing this on purpose...are you?"

I know, I know. It sounds a bit odd. But having other women in place who are dating just like you is important because they can give you a *wealth* of information in experiences, more than I could ever offer you in a single book.

It's not that you're looking for single women specifically. You're just looking for unmarried women your age who are involved in many active social circles. It's a foot in the door to meeting awesome people!

Where do you start? I recommend you set up profiles on all three of the following social sites designed specifically for women to meet other women in the area on a friendship basis:

- SocialJane.com

- GirlFriendCircles.com

- Girlfriend Social

"Ah, but Gregg, these are only for women without...without **friends**! Aren't they all weirdo's? What's wrong with them that they have no friends? I'd be embarrassed to be on one of those sites!"

Let's get one thing straight - women on these sites are in transition, *just like you are*. They're recently divorced, recently moved, recently lonely. They know there are other women out there to hang out with, but let's face it, it's not always easy to jump start a friendship on an elevator or in a shopping mall. These sites are *awesome* for getting to know people, *plus* they're very similar to dating sites, which we'll be going over in detail. You get to practice talking to people and setting up a cool profile without the stress of dating. There you go!

To go beyond women only sites, try Meetup.com. Meetup.com is bigger than all of the above sites combined, and you'll be able to meet both men and women on a *friendship basis*, usually in groups. Best of all, these are groups of people who share similar likes and hobbies. They might be a certain age, enjoy a certain activity or share a similar history. You can find people who enjoy wine tastings, dancing, fitness training, parenting or anything else you want!

The first meet up is the hardest. You'll be alone, you won't know anyone, and you'll either sink or swim. This is the only time I'll suggest taking a married friend who's willing to give you a push in the right direction. Once you meet people and you feel more comfortable, you won't need your friend to accompany you anymore.

Pick up a hobby you've always wanted to do. If you've read any of my other books, you know how big I am on hobbies and outside activities. While meeting friends for lunch incentivizes you to get out

Enjoy special gifts from your friends at

weightwatchers
reimagined

Find out how to get the
ebook or digital audiobook
of *The Path Made Clear*
for FREE!*

OFFER AVAILABLE AT
ww.com/ca/en/pmc

*EBOOK AND DIGITAL AUDIOBOOK OFFER
GOOD THROUGH JUNE 25. CANADA ONLY.

#PathMadeClear

Enjoy special gifts from your friends at

Receive a 50%* discount on a WW membership

there and *talk* to people, finding a hobby helps you to get out there *doing* things you love!

When you take on a hobby, what you're essentially doing is investing in yourself. You're saying you're worth the time - you're worth the *effort* of learning a new skill. This creates confidence, which in turn allows other people to see a more impressive "you."

The bonus is you're meeting people who share a similar passion! These people may be married, divorced, young, or old. What brings them together is their love of that hobby. It could be knitting, CrossFit, dancing—you name it, there's probably a group in your area doing it. Just Google® it and act on those search results!

I want you to act on at least one of these ideas right now. You can create a profile on one of those friendship sites, head over to Meetup.com, or Google a local class in your area. Before you go on another date, I want you to have a hobby in place *and* a friend or two who you go out with regularly. Before you know it you'll have a social life that makes you feel good about yourself, and will make you even *more* attractive to the men you date.

There's nothing sexier to a man than a woman who makes them work for each and every date. Staying busy is one of the key ingredients to getting an amazing guy.

The Makeover:
You Need to Feel Good to Look Good

No one can agree on what makes a woman attractive. Some men love large women, other men are attracted to Cosmo models who look like they haven't eaten in a month. You'll find guys who only want young girls, and guys who would rather date mature women who look and act like royalty.

It doesn't matter what "every guy" wants, because no woman could ever meet those requirements! What you want is a guy who is attracted to you when you *feel* your best, and in order to feel your best, you need to find *your* style.

I know you're going to hate what I say here ladies, but you need to get out there and treat yourself to a spa date! Go get a mani-pedi! Clean out your wardrobe and hit the shopping mall. Find what makes you *feel* sexy and wear it. I don't care if you have sexy lingerie and no one around who can appreciate it. The point is to wear it for **you**. Wear what makes you feel hot and you will become hot to the guys who are attracted to you in the first place!

Feeling good means feeling healthy, too.
Plenty of women can pull off sexy with a few extra pounds under their belts. Just look at Dana Elaine Owens, aka Queen Latifah. She's no twig, but what she has she makes work to her advantage. Kim Kardashian's butt alone weighs more than an entire catwalk model but she's one of the world's most

well-known sex symbols. Same goes for singer Amber Rose.

I'm sending you to Google® again! If you think you could stand to lose some pounds, go ahead and type in "plus size models" and check out the image results. Which body type approximates your own? Which body type would make you *feel* great without requiring you to starve yourself for months on end? Which body type could you conceivably achieve with a healthy eating lifestyle and a bit of exercise?

You can also get inspired by what men consider their top 10 plus-size models here: *http://www.ask men.com/top_10/celebrity/top-10-plus-size-models. html*. Which body type would make you feel most comfortable and sexy? Once you know what it is, find out the size and work toward it!

Remember, it's not about how *all guys* see you, it's about how the *right* guy sees you. **And the right guy is going to be attracted to how confident you pull off your body type.** If you spend months killing your-self for a size zero, then you'll be attracting guys who expect you to maintain that size. Are you sure you want to do that? Do you want to never eat another cupcake or chocolate bar again? If you choose that kind of guy and that kind of lifestyle, that's exactly where you'll be. All vanity and no cupcakes.

Confidence! I sound like a broken record but that's the key! Here's one of my favorite quotes from *Power of the Pussy*. Remember, this is written by a woman who weighs more than any Cosmo model, yet is far more confident in her own body (and thus makes better choices in *good* men).

> *"I don't care if you're the ugliest*
> *piece of shit walking the earth!*
> *You need to walk with your head up high*
> *and tell yourself you're beautiful."*

Hey, I didn't say it, but I freaking love it! She goes on to mention how it's not all about looks. You put forward other assets, whether it is a talent, a hobby, an accomplishment, etc. For the moment though, even if you don't feel comfortable in your own skin, you need to start saying you do. Telling yourself you're beautiful isn't going to make you believe it overnight, but as you're reaching for your ideal bodyweight and trying on a style that fits you, you'll start feeling more and more confident in what you can do and which guys you can have.

If you need an incentive other than looking great,
consider your health - even more important
It's more than just looks I'm talking about. Feeling healthy is essential, especially at this age. You're simply not going to feel healthy if the only thing you can fit into is a mumu. That's just asking for trouble down the road. Why not take the time now to truly revolutionize yourself. This is you 2.0 - a fresh start - and you want to feel great, which means *looking* great and being healthy.

Here's how to stay positive
while you work toward your size goal

You know what body size you want, and I hope you find a healthy way to get there. My recommendation is a combination of CrossFit lessons and portion control. I say CrossFit because you'll meet people who have similar weight-loss goals, which in turn motivates you to keep working at it. As for portion control, it doesn't require you to go on some crazy diet and as long as you follow through on the correct portions you'll start losing weight.

You can check out the Mayo Clinic for an excellent guide on portion control: *http://www.mayo clinic.org/healthy-living/weight-loss/multimedia/ portion-control/sls-20076148*. Alternatively, you could select a diet to go on, but make sure it's a diet you can really follow. Most dieters give up because they screw up on day and then it spirals out of control. Or they get to their goal weight and give up on the diet entirely. Diets suck. What you need are guidelines you can follow about how much you can eat, and then stay religious about it.

A second opinion from a younger generation

This is when it pays to have a college-aged daughter around. She'll have a pretty good idea about what's in style. More importantly, she can look you in the eye and say "Mom, I'll die of embarrassment if you go out on a date looking like that." Or "Mom, I swear, if you wear those granny panties, you better not be planning on inviting anyone in."

Second opinions are important. This is especially true if you've been a married mother for a decade or more. Somewhere along the line you stopped working as hard to look great. Things got too busy. When you barely have time to make your kids cereal in the morning before heading to the day job, it just stands to reason that wearing two mismatching shoes is the natural next step.

A college-aged daughter would do the trick here. I'd be a bit wary about going younger than that however. The younger generation walks a fine line between what's "in" and what's downright slutty. I think we've all seen those over-50 women at supermarkets sporting short jean skirts and dish-rag sized tube tops. Yikes!

Speak with the younger generation. Talk to them and show off the new clothing you find, but at the same time, own your age! Stay true to you just as you are. Get recommendations from both younger women and women your age. Find a blend you love and make it your style. Sure it's going to take some trial and error, but you're going to find that perfect style!

You Have Everything You Need to Go on Amazing Dates

If you've followed the advice in Chapters 1 and 2, you're all set to hit the dating scene. You've kicked your fears and baggage to the curb, you've gotten rid of habits that you acquired after years of married life, and you've acquired some new friends and a new social life along the way.

Let's get specific and outline exactly what we learned in Chapter 2:

- Confidence is the most important tool in your tool box. With confidence, you'll be resilient enough to fight off the fears of rejection, and you'll never settle when it comes to your dating life.

- Your fears have no basis in reality. You could be in your 40's, 50's, 60's, and older, and *still* land an amazing guy. Men of all ages want to date you. You're hot stuff and you need to realize it.

- You're your own worst enemy. You need to embrace change, work towards it **today**, build up a routine and reward yourself when you succeed.

- Confidence comes when *you* define your own life. If you let a man define it, you'll always lack confidence, and your man will not treat you with respect. To overcome this, meet new people! Join MeetUp groups and find activities you love. You'll have fun **plus** you'll be even more desirable to the right kind of men (the men who are looking for women with value.)

- Get fit, find the body type that you feel great in, and work towards it. Eat healthy, join work-out groups, and focus on **you**, not what others think of you. Remember, the skinniest models in the world can feel zero confidence. It's all about feeling confident in your own skin.

I feel that you need two very important skills before you start dating again: Confidence in Yourself and an Understanding of the Male Mind. I provide both because I am a life coach and a male dating coach. I have two rockin' paid courses with tons of videos with me if you are interested.

Understand Men Here:

https://who-holds-the-cards-now.thinkific.com/ courses/the-man-whisperer

Find Confidence Here:

https://who-holds-the-cards-now.thinkific.com/ courses/build-yourself-and-he-will-come/

Chapter 3:
It's Raining Men!
How to Land a First Date Fast

Confidence? *Check*. Social Life? *Check*. Freedom? *Check!* It's time to go on some dates!

"Whoa, **whoa there** Gregg! I just wouldn't know where to start. I don't know what I'm looking for in a guy, and even if I did, where do I find him? It's not like I bump into guys every day at Walmart. And heck, even if I *landed* a date with an awesome guy, I wouldn't know how to act around him!"

Hey, relax! I'm going to take you step by step through every one of those questions. By the end of Chapter 3, you'll have first dates lining up around the block! If not I'll come date you myself!

To Find the Right Man,
You Need to Define Him for Yourself First

Grab a pen and some paper ladies.

You have a chance to really find a great guy this time around. I mean it! If you follow the steps I mentioned in Chapters 1 and 2, then you are **worthy** of an amazing man.

If you don't think you're worthy of a good guy, I want you to put that pen and notebook away, read over Chapters 1 and 2 again, and get to work building your confidence. That confidence is your golden ticket. Without it, you'll *never* meet Mr. Right... you'll just keep meeting Mr. I-Guess-He'll-Do, or Mr. He-Wasn't-Who-I-Thought-He-Was.

You've already been down that road! Did you know 67% of second marriages fail, and 73% of *third* marriages fail? You'd think people learn from their mistakes, but instead they're **doubling down** on them!

First get the confidence you need, *and then* define your man.

What are you looking for in a man?

Okay, grab that pen and paper again. We're doing this.

Briefly write down five things you want a guy to have. This could be something related to looks, money, emotions, whatever. Write down the five most essential things you'd like a guy to have.

Got it? Good. Now write down the five biggest deal breakers, the five things would make you run for the hills the minute you noticed it in a man. These should come as quickly as possible. Don't pause to think about it. Write them down fast.

At this point you have your five requirements and your five deal breakers. Now, over the next week, I want you to expand your list, writing five more requirements and five more deal breakers. Really think about these. When they come to you over the course of the week, write them in. Don't scratch out the initial 5 in each category. Regardless of how much thought you put into this list later, those initial 5 must stay.

The goal here is simple. As you go on dates, label guys on a 1-to-10 scale based on how many of those requirements you think they meet. This isn't easy to do after a single date. You'll need more than one to really get a fix on a guy. Until you can rate him however, you are *honor bound* to see him without emotional blinders on! Even if the guy seems completely awesome on your first and second dates, you must maintain your composure, put on the cold hard mask of reason, and rate that guy based on your list.

Alternatively, if he shows even **one** of the deal breakers, he's done. Gone. Finished.

Note - there's a reason why I want you to rate each guy on a requirement-based 1-to-10 scale, rather than judge them based on the requirements which you find most important on your list. This is to make sure you go on dates with different KINDS of guys - guys who you may have ignored or overlooked previously.

I'll give you an example. Let's say you hold looks as a huge requirement. If you could number this list from 1-10, looks would be first on the list. Chances are, if looks is your #1 requirement, you may ignore *all* of your other requirements, just for a chance to date this super-hot guy.

On a 1-to-10 scale, that super-hot guy may score a 2- or 3-out-of-10, but you don't care because he's the hottest dude you've ever seen! Meanwhile, you turn down a date with a guy who may have been lacking a bit in the looks department, but he was a straight up 8 or 9 on your requirement scale! Who do you think is going to last longer?

Hey, if you love dating hot guys, then get out there and date them! But you need to separate the 1's and 2's and 3's from the actual decent guys who you want to spend the rest of your life with. Have fun while you're dating, but don't get blinded by just one or two requirements.

Follow your list, not your heart

Yes, you heard me right. Your heart will deceive you. For some guys, giving you butterflies in your stomach is as easy as turning on a light switch. They know how to manipulate a woman's emotions, and guess what? You'll either get used or be stuck with a guy who has three, four, five or even **more** of your deal breakers. But hey, he's hot right? So you get married, spend 5 years figuring all of this out, and then whammo, divorce #2. Ouch.

If you have a history of dating bad guys, this is even more important.

I don't want to get into the psychology of why you make bad choices in men. That's not important. What's important is that you break out of those choices right now! And you'll never accomplish this when you keep justifying a guy's behavior because you like being around him. No more settling!

Let's get even more specific

Of all the online dating sites today, I feel like eHarmony has the most detailed "compatibility" guide. You've probably filled out one of these guides before if you've dated online. It's basically a massive list of questions that you need to answer before you have access to a site's matchmaking services. When you fill out a guide like this, it helps match you to people with similar personality traits and interests. Fun stuff!

What I want you to do is log on to eHarmony, set up a free trial, and fill out that compatibility guide. You're going to be completely inundated with questions about who you are and what you're looking for. When you see something that you feel is very meaningful, write it down! This will help clarify your search and hone in on the exact kind of man you're looking for.

Even more specific than that?

Here's a tip I really think helps women visualize the kind of guy they want. I want you to hit up an additional dating website or two, set up your profile (we'll talk about how to set up the perfect profile in a bit, so if you want, just set up a fake one for now and delete it later) and start browsing profiles of the men on there.

What immediately jumps out at you? What makes you think that guy would be a great match for you? Is it a personality trait you have in common? Do you share certain hobbies? Do you have the same work ethic? When something really jumps out at you, write it down! And as you start dating in earnest, you can rearrange these ideas into the right order, from the most important, to the least important.

Follow the above tips to really get a feel for who you are and what you're looking for in a man. Use the 1-to-10 scale because it helps you see the *real* value of a man, **not** just his charm and good looks. And lastly, don't get *too* detailed regarding your "perfect man." I highly doubt you'll find a 10/10, let alone a 10/10 who also shares the many personality traits, hobbies, facial features, and enjoyments which you wrote down while checking out profiles online. Finding a great guy means giving him some leeway, too. Otherwise you may really miss out on Mr. Right!

Men Are Everywhere
(You Just Need to Know Where to Look)

"Gregg, can I just stop you right now? Let's be serious here. Even if I know the kind of guy I'm looking for, he's never going to go for me. He's going to go for those hot 20- or 30-something's. That's great if you think guys are all over the place, but they sure aren't looking for *me*."

I can't wait to prove you wrong! Beating out your younger competition is **easy**, and I'll show you why right now.

Let me explain. One of my favorite things to do is check out online dating sites because they contain so many hidden gems of information. On SugarDaddie for example, a site for wealthy men looking for women, you have gorgeous young women who only bother to show off their good looks. That's it. That's their claim to fame.

So is this enough for the men on SugarDaddie? Not by a long shot. Sure it will suffice for men who are looking for sex alone. But those aren't the kinds of guys you're looking for! The younger crowd is doing you a favor by getting rid of all the sharks. Now you have your pick of the great guys.

While I was browsing SugarDaddie I came across this hilarious exchange between this hot 23-year-old and a rich stockbroker she was trying to woo (I changed his name for privacy purposes). Tell me if this isn't the funniest thing you've ever read:

Hi Jim, take a look and contact me. I'm the real deal!

Her Profile:

I'm extremely attractive and have expensive tastes. I like travel, shopping and enjoy fine wines. I will only settle for someone who can afford this lifestyle. I'm seeking a long term relationship leading to marriage and kids. I model in NYC currently and I will happy to send you more pics if you make the cut. And by the way, NYC is not cheap! Please, my time is valuable and I will not play games. Are you my man?

Thank you

Dreams do come true

His Response:

Dear Miss Dreams do come true,

Thank you for contacting me. And yes, you are the real deal – very beautiful indeed! I meet your criteria with flying colors – I make millions. My problem is this: I will continue to make more and more money while your beauty will fade. I look at this like a business deal and anyone in my shoes would be foolish to marry you. You are a depreciating asset while my assets will grow exponentially.

My advice to you would be to stop trying to sell yourself with your looks and concentrate on intriguing us with your personality. We are not stupid, we did not get where we are with bad decisions so why would we start now?

Sincerely,
Jim Larson

Ladies, you need to realize quality men want your *personality*. To them, personality IS beauty. Given, if you're 60 and still gorgeous, then great! But we both know you (and I) will not look as great we do now 10, 15, 20 years down the road.

Again, older men do not want younger women in their 20's and 30's to settle down with. I'm the perfect example of this mentality. I've dated younger women in their 30's and I'm over that phase. Yes, I know there are exceptions, but I'm talking about quality men. When a man falls in love, really falls in love, a woman's beauty only increases with age. So rest assured, the type of man you want is not interested in some young bimbo!

The Offline Scene: Meeting Men in the Real World

Ladies, it's time to jump back into the bar scene!

Just kidding.

You don't need to set foot into a bar, or any place is rampant with 20- and 30-something's. It's not you anymore. Many of my female clients find the bar scene disappointing and superficial, which it is! You just don't realize it until later on in life.

Again, we don't need to go pretending we're not the age we are. Different needs need to be met in your 40's, 50's and 60's. The club scene is out. You want a guy who's going to wine and dine you, make you laugh and make you feel great.

How do we go about finding this army of single men? What are they doing? What are their interests, where are they hanging out? Let's talk about some of the places where my clients have found the best luck.

- **Charity events:** Charity events are great places to mingle with interesting single men. In most cases these men are well off, engaged in a social cause and have a solid educational background. Go with a few friends to avoid feeling out of place.

- **Casinos and resort hotels:** Take some girl-friends and head to the casino scene. No slots, no bingo—I want you to head straight to the blackjack or roulette tables. Trust me, if you pick a table and stay there, guys will see you. If you find yourself standing next to some-one interesting, ask them friendly questions about the game (even if you know all about it) to get the ball rolling on a conversation.

- **Dog parks:** Don't have a dog? Borrow one. Then head out to a dog park which you know is hopping with people. Single guys are **everywhere** in parks like these. The best part is you have an instant conversation starter (hint: it's the dog you borrowed from your next door neighbor).

- **Local live music events:** Obviously you'll need to be picky here. Many of these live music events are at bars, but you'll want to find the ones going on at the premier spots. You know...the ones with $15 martinis? Applebee's just isn't going to cut it here (but by all means, hanging out at an Applebee's bar isn't the worst place to meet men.)

- **Public travel:** You'll have to get creative with your conversation starters, but I'm not joking, public transportation offers a great place to meet men! Conversation starters include commenting on something he's reading or saying something about how busy it is. You can also "accidentally" drop something next to him.

- **Singles cruises:** You're on a boat with tons of single men. How much better can it get? This removes any fear of speaking to a taken man. At the same time, you'll want to avoid the guys who are there just for the sex. If he presses you too much in this regard, kindly decline and move on.

- **Golf lessons:** Older guys love their golf. They also usually have cash and a stable job, since this is not an inexpensive sport. Take a friend and set up a lesson schedule. Afterwards, head to the course's restaurant and hang out for an afternoon cocktail.

There are tons of other places you can find men, but the above often hold the most promise. I'd also check out local restaurants, grocery stores, and even hardware stores. You do not need to show your hand right away that what you're looking for is a date. Just play it cool, ask him a question, and if a conversation starts to flow naturally from it, keep it going and see where it leads. No embarrassment at all!

The Online Scene: Yes, You Need to Be Here

No dating eBook is complete these days without a discussion on online dating. I know, all of this seemed to just happen overnight. Maybe you were married, busy with kids, busy with your job, and didn't think much of it. Today however, I want you to reconsider. Online dating is **the** best way to find a great guy.

No joke. The stigma is gone. More people than ever before are trying it. You **need** to be online trying it too. Why? Because you can vet guys right away, you have TONS of guys to choose from, and best of all, you don't have to go on a real date until you're ready.

What dating sites should I use?

There are dozens of great dating websites out there. The really big ones that you've heard of (eHarmony, Match.com, OK Cupid) are excellent due to the sheer volume of people coming and going. You should set up profiles for all three of these sites, if only to browse profiles and get a feel for who's out there.

Alternatively, niche dating sites have fewer members, but those members who are on the site share very similar interests or hobbies. For example, if you love horses, try EquestrianSingles.com. Want someone who shares your political views? Try RepublicanPeopleMeet.com or DemocraticPeopleMeet.com. Looking for someone around your age bracket? Try OurTime.com. Want someone to mess around with? Try Tinder.com, or AshleyMadison.com.

My suggestion would be to select 5 dating sites which you really like, and then create profiles for each one of them. In this way, you have a huge pool of men available to you, and therefore more chances to find someone you really like.

Creating Your Profile

A lot of women I've helped tend to feel overwhelmed by their profiles. They either don't know how to answer the profile questions or they can't seem to find a picture which represents them the way they'd like. Some end up putting off their profiles or giving up entirely.

We aren't going to do that. What **we're** going to do is answer each question honestly and in a relaxed way, as if no one is going to be looking at it! Forget the guys for a second. Right now, you're sharing your honest opinion, just to yourself, about the kind of person you are, and the kind of person you'd like to meet. Keep your responses short and don't go on tangents.

I'd recommend looking at women's profiles until you find one you absolutely love. Then, copy that same "style" and tone of voice in your own profile. It's not called cheating. It's called getting inspired ☺

Once your finished writing, go over all of your answers and make sure of three things:

1. There aren't any grammar/punctuation mistakes

2. Limit the amount of "I's" you have in your profile. No one wants to read a monologue.

3. Make sure you remove ALL negative comments about yourself from your profile

That third point is important. Your profile is not the place to make light of yourself or demean yourself in any way. Remember, you're **confident** and you're **accomplished**. If you go bashing yourself or saying little things like "I know I look fat in that picture," or "I hate that I haven't traveled much, but I want to!" then you're going to attract men who feed off of your insecurities and take advantage of you.

Again, when you find a negative, **chop it**. Find a way to turn it into a positive. Don't say "I've got two kids and they're a handful so I never know how much time I'll have." Instead, say "I've got two kids and they're the love of my life. I want a man who respects how much I love them and maybe even has some of his own."

Regarding your picture, if you simply cannot find one you want on your profile page, then seek out a professional photographer. Consider it an investment toward your future, which is exactly what it is. The more confident you feel about your profile, the better choices you'll make in the men who come calling.

Here are a few more profile creation tips you'll want to remember!

•   **Have your kids help out!** Yes, your kids are a wealth of information when it comes to the online world. They'll help you find the sites you need and will even be brutally honest with you about what you should and shouldn't say.

- **Save all of your profile information in a Microsoft Word document.** This way you can cut and paste your responses into other dating websites.

- **Delete your profile from time to time and start fresh.** By that, I don't mean recreate your entire profile. What I mean is if you delete your profile and start fresh, the site will rank you as "new," which means you'll be on their front page, where everyone can see you!

- **Don't sound too sexual on your profile.** Don't make it sound like you're just looking for sex. You can talk about fun things you can both do together, but avoid sexual innuendo.

- **Don't make any demands on your profile.** So don't start off by saying "I want a guy who's got money and a good job." Or, "I need someone who is committed to me and my kids." That's just going to scare guys away!

Play the field!

You've selected your dating websites and you've written up your profiles. Great! Now it's time to kick up your feet and let the guys come to you.

Orrrrr, maybe not. "Gregg, I just set up my profile and no one is writing me. Am I doing something wrong??"

Maybe, or maybe you just haven't given yourself enough time yet. Some of the niche sites don't have a lot of members, so it may take more time for a guy to contact you. Also, did you set up profiles on more than one site? If not, you need to get on that. It's all about playing the field and seeing which website gets you the most success.

Have you followed all of my profile advice? Are you making demands in your profile, or saying bad things about yourself?

Lastly, and this one's important: are *you* going to *them*?

The online world is a bit different from the offline world. In the online world, a woman can go ahead and hit that "poke" button, "wink" button, "flirt" button or whatever button you have available! If you see a guy you think is date material, send him a brief message telling him you liked his profile and would enjoy speaking to him over the phone.

One thing to note: you can make the first move in the online dating world, but once the initial conversation starts, *he* needs to pursue *you*.

Last but not least, stay safe

Life is full of whack-jobs and con artists and they love taking advantage of women in whatever way possible. **Always** vet your man before you go on a date with him. Talk to him over the phone first and never give out your personal information right away. When you go out on a first date, go to some place **public**, *not* his house. I know this sounds silly to even be talking about this, but bad things happen to gullible women on the internet.

Here's an example: in one of the most bizarre stories I've ever heard, Suzanne Hardman, a recently-widowed middle-aged woman from the UK, gave her **entire life savings**, over $200,000, to a group of 6 conmen masquerading as one "James Richards" on Match.com. They kept the lie going for almost a year. By the time Mrs. Hardman figured it out, she had given almost everything she had to this "man" whom she had never met.

Her "friend" James Richards kept saying his father had millions stashed away in a bank in India, and he didn't have the money to pay the inheritance tax to get it out. He even went so far as to send her falsified bank documents. I know the whole thing sounds crazy, but trust me, *it happens more than you think*. Never date a guy who you can't meet in under a couple of hours, and **never** give money to someone who you've never met.

Enough of all of the grim stuff. Even though it happens, it's not going to happen to you. Why? Because now you're smart, you know better and you're going to use online dating to find a great man, not a weirdo or con artist.

You Landed Your First Date!
Here's How to Make Sure It's Awesome

You've done it! You've snagged a first date with a guy who seems to be a great match! Now you have the dreaded first date staring you in the face. Somewhere along the way, the first date has gotten a bad rap. It has become something we fear and look to with great anticipation and dread.

This is not common to you women either! We men have just as much anxiety about this first date as you do, perhaps more. We also want to look good, smell good, and come off as being intelligent and not flakey.

Even if you're going out with someone you have met before informally, the "first date" is a prickly situation. Where should you go? What should you wear? Should you use this cologne or that one? Get your nails done or don't? Do you drink? Do you eat? Lean forward, slouch, be board stiff? What *do* you do?

Fear not, your old pal Gregg is here for you! We're going to walk through the first date in a way that has you striding confidently into that scene. He'll be drooling from the first second he sees you and he'll *definitely* be calling you for another!

First off—Where to go
Many people choose a restaurant, pub or coffee house for a first date. This can lead to many awkward moments. When you're in a food-based

environment, there are always unanswered questions like:

- Should I drink?

- Should I order a second drink?

- Should I let him buy my coffee?

- Are we here for dinner or just drinks?

- If I eat, should I get just a salad?

There are tons of questions which produce even more anxiety, and if you *do* get past these, there are the inevitable conversation and dead air issues which come from being in an otherwise stagnant environment. Most of these ideas offer you some more natural ways to initiate conversation and also offer the ability to step away for a moment or two if you need a breather.

Rather than go to a food place, try one of these ideas:

- Go bowling

- Go to the zoo or aquarium

- Visit an art museum

- Attend a festival or fair

- Go to a wine tasting

- Go golfing – even putt-putt

- Do something activity based like a bike ride, a hike, or even a yoga class

- Go to a sporting event, like a baseball or hockey game

- Go to the theater

- Catch a local band

- Go to a comedy club

- Check out your town – act like you're sight seers for a day

- If it's the holiday season and you live in a town which has great window displays, go "window shopping"

- Go ice skating, roller skating or roller blading

- Try out a cooking, pottery, or other type of class (offer to pay your half)

- Go for a walk (in a very public place, not the woods!)

- Go for a canoe or paddle boat ride, or even boating if you can

- Volunteer somewhere together

- Go to a bookstore

- Go to an auction

- Go to a dog park

- Go dancing

- Visit an amusement park

- Go someplace photograph-worthy and focus on taking great pictures

- Ask your date to teach you something in an area in which he excels

- Take a hot air balloon ride

If you're looking for something a little edgier, consider going star-gazing or having dinner in the dark. The important thing is to take the focus off of sitting and staring at one another by adding an element of fun, adventure or mystery. Try to suggest things which you know may interest your date, not just yourself, and be open to his suggestions too. Even if you've never done something before, it doesn't mean you can't try it now! If nothing else, you gain a new experience in life which you can add to your repertoire!

What to wear

What you wear on a date will depend on what type date you decide to try. Don't put on your best heels and pencil skirt to go bowling or hiking. It's okay to show up in jeans and a comfy sweatshirt if that's what the date suggests. Just be mindful of a few things. First off, choose clothing that doesn't say "I'm planning to have sex with you later." This means keeping cleavage to a minimum and avoiding mini-skirts are shorter than your 6-inch stilettoes.

Don't wear things which are dirty or have holes in them (yes I mean *those* jeans).

Okay I know I said be comfy, but I didn't mean pick the sweatshirt which has holes at the top of the pocket or where the ribbing attaches. Jeans with holes are just not first date material either. Even if you bought them that way, don't wear 'em for this date!

Be true to yourself. Don't borrow your best friend's hot red dress! Wear something comfortable which you own! If you're planning to attend a black-tie event, then you're going to need that nice black dress (notice I didn't say little black dress (refer to item 1). Even then, be comfortable. If you're con-stantly tugging at something or hiking up your shirt, we will be distracted.

Wear flattering colors. Ask your friends or family what colors look good on you and build a wardrobe which has those colors, at least as highlights. Men are visual creatures. If your skin is snow-pale and you show up in something which washes you out even further, our first impression may not be all that great.

Avoid the 'expensive' wardrobe look. If you show up with all of your Prada, Gucci and Coach Labels hanging out, we'll mark you as high maintenance and shut down. Even if you bought those things for yourself, it sends a message. Yes, you look great, but men don't notice labels unless you smack us in the head with them. Don't worry about who made it, just worry about how it looks on you!

Show-Off What You've Got. I know, I said don't flash skin earlier, but that doesn't mean you put on a baggy potato sack of an outfit which camouflages your assets. We still need to see the curves, just let us *imagine* what they look like without the clothes for now!

Save Crazy for Later. We know you have some 'out there' outfits which you like to put on now and then, but don't wear 'em on the first date unless this is really who you are! Even if it's the most comfortable thing you own, please save your wild side for another day.

"But Gregg, he invited me to a big event." Relax, just ask him what you should wear. He doesn't expect you to intuitively know that it's really an ugly sweater party or a black tie event. He'd rather show up with someone he can show off than someone he wants to hide in the closet. He will even like that you're taking the extra step to make sure you look good. If it's some sort of gala or other type of event where pictures might be online, check out what folks have worn in the past.

What to say

If you thought finding something to wear was difficult, trying to figure out what to say—or what *not* to say—can be downright terrifying. I've provided you with a few things you need to make sure you fit into the conversation.

Say "thank you." Thank your date for meeting you, even if you didn't have a good time. If the date went well, this just puts a notch in your cap for a next date. If it didn't, it's still polite to thank him.

"Next time we get together...." This is better than "can we do this again sometime?" because it shows hope, rather than a lack of confidence or uncertainty. For example, "next time we get together, you pick the place" or "you bowl first." Whatever fits the situation—think context!

Stick to positive topics. Even if your grandmother just passed a couple of weeks ago, don't dwell on it for a first date. If you're that torn up, maybe you should postpone the date. Men don't want to be on a downer date. Stay on positive topics, and if a topic comes up which stirs a negative memory, make a brief comment and redirect the conversation to something else.

"I like you." Why not spare the mystery? If you like

the guy, let him know. Remember, he's nervous too. This could open up a next date conversation too! You could try saying it like this, "You know what Tim? I might just take you out again!" See how easy and fun that is? You just said, "I like you" but you exude confidence in the way you said it...*Brilliant!*

"Let's Try....[insert adventure here]" Don't be afraid to show your adventurous side! For example, if you're someplace where people are dancing, then offer up a dance. He may want to ask you, but he's probably afraid he'll come off as being too forward.

Be a good listener. As he shares information about himself, be a good listener and provide honest and natural feedback to what he's saying. Even if it's a topic you're not very familiar with, you can dig up something to say. For example, if he starts talking about football, but you don't know a football from a basketball, then find a way to turn some of what he said around and repeat it ("ah yeah, I heard that the 49'ers are having a bad year somewhere too!") Follow up with a topic change that you're more comfortable with when he's finished.

"You're very interesting." If you find him interesting, tell him. Compliments on a date don't just go one way! It helps us know what to talk about with you in the future. By the same token, if we're talking about something you know nothing about, kindly let us know – something like "Well, I've never thought much about improvements to football helmets before" tells us to steer clear of that one with you.

"You have great taste in shirts" (or pants or shoes or whatever). This is a shade better than "you look good tonight" because it really points out that he tried to dress nicely. This can be an opener for conversation about something in your comfort zone too – shopping. He might even come back with something amusing like "yeah, I dragged my secretary out with me to help me choose this shirt."

"Have you ever been to...[insert place]." This can be someplace local, like your favorite pub, or it can be someplace like another country if you know your date is a traveler. In the same way, if he's interested in music, ask if he's ever been to a concert for a local band. Whatever the interest area, you can have a "have you ever been to" type of question, especially if you *have* been there!

3 _What not to say_

Okay, along with what *to* say is what *not* to say! There are some things which just shouldn't be said on a first date, or any date for that matter. These things are date-killers. Avoid them at all cost!

"I'm not looking for a relationship." Buzz Kill! We're already turned off. We are probably dating to find a great girl to have a relationship with, so if you don't want a relationship, a first date is not the place to announce it – in fact, why are you *on* a first date anyway?

"The last guy I dated...." This is not the time to tell us you're comparing us to your last failed relationship. We want to hear about you, not some other guy who fell short. Save that stuff for your girlfriends.

"You look different than your profile picture." Different how? Fatter, skinnier, balder, more hair, teeth too yellow? Observe it, but we don't need to hear it. We probably already know this anyway, we don't need to hear your disappointment, shock or surprise.

"I want to know everything about you – and conversely – let me tell you everything you need to know about me." This is intimidating. We don't want to *tell* you everything about us on a first date, and we don't want to hear everything about you either. Allow for mystery to remain after the first date – on both sides.

"I'm nervous." This is sort of a 'duh' statement. Of course you're nervous – so are we. Unfortunately, we'll probably end up pitying you, which equates to no second date.

"You're not the type of person I usually go for."

This is going to leave us wondering two things: why are we here and what type of person *do* you usually go for? Even if it's meant as a compliment, it's a big **no**. Instead of saying this, try noting something about us that you find unique or interesting, like "I love how passionate you are about animals!"

"How long have you been on [insert dating site]." This is just plain awkward. If we've only been on there for a little while, it might seem as if we're inexperienced. If we've been on the site for months, it might make us look like there's something wrong with us.

"Do you go on a lot of dates?" Depending on how old the guy is, this could be bad either way. If a guy is 40 and says no, you might think he's inexperienced, when the truth is he married his high school sweetheart who recently died of cancer.

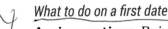

What to do on a first date

Arrive on time. Being late, especially on a first date, is not only disrespectful, it also causes your guy to have an unnecessary level of anxiety. He's already nervous and now you've left him wondering if you're even coming. You're also taking a chance that he'll even wait for you.

Let him know you're having a good time. We're trying to impress you and we want you to enjoy the date. Don't be afraid to tell us you're enjoying yourself. Chances are, your guy will breathe a huge sigh of relief and will probably relax a little bit. It might even open up a conversation for what to do on the next date!

Be yourself. Don't try to be the woman you think we want to date. Instead, be yourself. Whether we met you through an online dating service, a friend, or another situation, we've already found something about you which has piqued our interest. Pretending to be someone you're not will eventually catch up with you anyway, so just be you.

Echo. Pay attention to what he's doing and echo some of his behaviors. For example, if he leans into the conversation, you can lean in a little bit too. This type of action on your part (echoing) gives the impression that you are in sync with one another.

Dig deeper. It's easy to stay on surface topics during a first date, but if you find common ground, dig deeper. This will help to spark a great conversation and you'll avoid that painful, deadly silence. The conversation also won't feel forced or fake.

Use body language. Be aware of good and bad body language. Use body language which is open and inviting, such as leaning in to the conversation. Be aware of the signals you are sending with things like crossing your arms in front of you, which suggests you are unapproachable.

Share a funny story. While your fella doesn't want to hear your life story, sharing a funny story might help to break the ice. Even a funny story about a past first date will do. He probably has a story to share too and then you begin to find common ground!

Offer to pay your portion. While we're often more than happy to pay for you, it's certainly a nice gesture to offer to pay for your own part of the date. Don't be offended if we say okay either – we like you didn't come into it with a sense of entitlement. If we offer to pay, toss out there "okay I owe you a coffee the next time then" or something similar.

S *Things not to do*

Get on your phone. We don't know what you're doing on your phone. You could be texting another guy, sharing how awful you think the date is with your friends or talking to your kids. Try to make arrangements for your kids to reach out to someone else first if possible. If you must have your phone out because of kids, let your guy know and don't use it for anything else.

Get drunk. I've covered this before, but it's worth repeating. Don't get drunk – I don't care how nervous you are. A glass of wine or two is okay if it doesn't make you tipsy.

Talk about all of your ailments. We aren't inter-ested in your medical history and telling us about all of the drugs you take won't exactly endear us to you either. Certainly if you're out to eat and there is something you need to avoid, let us know, but other-wise, keep it to yourself.

Bring up sex. Talking about sex on the first date is just a no-no. You already know from reading my other books that sex on a first date is taboo, don't tell us about your preferences and good or bad experiences just now. It will distract us from the real purpose of the date, which is getting to know you better (but not *that* much better!)

Talk about subjects which are too deep. Stay away from conversations about marriage, children and family. We are here to get to know you, but we don't want to talk marriage on this date. That's waaaaaaaaaaaay down the line conversation-wise. Talking about this now will only freak us out and send us running in another direction.

Discuss finances. While your finances are import-ant to your guy, talking about them now is not appro-priate. We can pick up on enough signals about your financial situation to tide us over for now.

Wander off to chat with a friend. If you see some-one you know, a simple wave is probably good enough. Don't go off and have a fifteen-minute con-versation with someone else. You're on a date with your guy, not out with a girlfriend. If they choose to walk over to the table and say hello, the conversa-tion will likely last just a minute or two.

Lie. I've said this before, but I need to say it again. Don't lie. Whether you're embellishing or flat out telling a ginormous fib, just don't do it. These things always catch up with you and, in the end, are worse than the truth would have been in the beginning.

You Have Everything You Need to Make Your First Date Work

A long chapter, but an important one! At this point, you have a ton of tricks up your sleeve when it comes to knowing what you want, where to find what you want and what to do on a first date to make sure you nail it.

Some key points for Chapter 3:

- Follow your 1-to-10 list and rate men based off of their number. If you simply give yourself a list and rank each requirement by importance, you'll likely only pick a guy based on the top 3 or even top 1. You'll end up picking a guy for his looks, rather than another guy who wasn't as good looking but had everything else.

- Use dating website compatibility guides and

check out profiles of guys to get a better idea of what type of guy interests you.

- When it comes to offline dating, make sure you're avoiding bars and trying more refined spots, like high-end casinos, resorts, and charity events.

- When it comes to online dating, you have a **huge** selection of websites to choose from. Don't be shy, create more than one profile!

- **Be Safe!** Protect yourself. Never meet a man in a private place and never send money or divulge private information to a man you've never met.

- Your first date will be both nerve-wracking and fun! Use my tips and I guarantee you'll be fantastic.

Chapter 4:
Dating for Keeps:
Attraction, Flirting,
& Finding an Awesome Guy

The kid gloves are coming off in Chapter 4. By this point you have everything you need to jump into the dating scene. Your baggage is handled, you know what you're looking for, and you know where to find great guys. And most importantly of all, you're confident. You're excited to see who's out there for you!

Chapter 4 is the final piece of the puzzle. By the end of this chapter, you'll know how to weed out the bad guys who aren't going anywhere, how to get comfortable with dating more than one person at a time, and above all, how to get guys to **beg** you for another date.

But that's enough for one introduction. Let's get started with Chapter 4!

Have Them Begging to Date You Again

Ladies, you have more power over men than you realize. If you wanted to, you could get a man to do almost anything for you. No joke, anything you want. He'll give it to you.

Does this sound like your life so far? No? That's fine. What you need is already innate within you.

You *know* how to make a man sweat, to get him right where you want him. What hides this innate ability is a lack of confidence. A woman with extreme confidence will turn any man into putty. Women with confidence will *melt* any man.

But what, exactly, does a man *notice* which makes a woman seem confident? Let's go over some of the key facts about how a guy identifies a confident woman.

#1: She is busy. A confident woman is naturally busy. No faking it here, she has her own career, hobbies and friends who demand her attention. The man will know this when he asks her out, she will need to tell **him** the few times when she's available.

#2: She is interesting. This is where everything comes together. She's busy with her hobbies and her hobbies make her interesting. Think about it, when a woman can explain exactly how to ride a wave in the middle of winter during a rare hurricane in New England with a short board...she becomes very confident in a man's eyes. Now I picked surfing, but the reality is it doesn't matter. I'm amazed when a woman explains how she gets the wick of a candle inside the wax and makes it smell so friggin' good!

#3: She challenges him and has her own opinion. This is huge sign of a confident woman to a man. "Rest Stops" are 'yes' girls. "Keepers" have opinions and they express them! Rest Stops go along with whatever the man says. Their schedules are always free, and they just agree with what he says because they don't have any experience in the field of whatever the subject is at hand. When a man starts talking politics he doesn't want the woman to look at him glassy eyed and say "Uh, what?" No, he wants her to come back and express her opinion about her side and her views. Now obviously she won't know everything but he won't either! Thus, the conversation becomes a give and take (a learning experience) between both and becomes ***interesting!***

#4: She has boundaries. If a man is late constantly, doesn't call when he should or he attempts to sleep with her too soon – there will be consequences. Many men will test these boundaries and they will receive no resistance. Next morning, it's "bye-bye." Confident women, needless to say, will soon be showing these men the door.

#5: She has money. Yes, I said it – confident women have money! I always receive some kick back on this one but it's true. Don't come to me with 10k in credit card debt and a beat up 96 Honda leaking oil. I don't care how hot you are! Now, of course there are exceptions – I get it. But I'm talking about women in general. There's no reason not to have a reasonable job which allows you to get off daddy's allowance at age 35. Financials are important and many women seek the guy to take care of the issue, and that is where we say, "hasta la vista." Remember, we are looking for the woman of our dreams too – we need a woman who has some sort of respect towards their own income!

#6: She rarely gets jealous. Confident women don't compare themselves to other women because they're comfortable in their own shoes. They know they are beautiful inside and very unique. She never has to worry about a guy checking out other women in front of her because she would never date a guy like this! If, by accident, she went on a date with a guy like this, she would never go out with him again. Not because she's jealous, but because she knows he's not worthy of her time – big difference.

Now I know all guys check out other women, but I'm talking about someone who does it consistently in front of their significant other.

#7: She allows her guy to take control. Yes, she realizes men want to provide by paying at times, opening car doors and helping her. She allows this behavior because she is smart as a fox and knows she'll be rewarded in many other ways going forward. Allowing a man to provide makes him feel complete and keeps his eyes on the prize, which is you! Many older, successful women don't quite get this and they emasculate a man without even realizing it by always wearing the boots.

Ladies, hammer these seven things above home! Before any date, rehearse these items over and over! If you can hold your own on these, you will never have another man break up with you again!

Want to see him drop all pretenses to impress you?
Okay, date more guys! P P Y

This is a big one and I often beat it to death. Never go all in with a man until he has proven himself. Many older women are just getting back out there and are happy with the first man who is breathing. Stop! These first men should be your lab rats to test things on, not your soulmates! I would like you to fill your koi pond with many koi **before** you start making choices.

Date 10 guys, not all at once, but maybe two or three at a time. Experience a guy you thought you'd never date and make the decision based on experience and not what your best friend or 90-year-old mother recommends. This gives you choices and comparison. **Furthermore, the guys you're dating know you have options so they step up their game because they know you're a higher value woman with confidence.**

Again, no matter what happens, whether you like a guy or not, whether you follow up with a guy on a second date or not, you'll need to date at least 10 guys before taking any action to pursue a long-term relationship with one of them.

"But Gregg, what if I *really* like the first guy I date...why go on other dates with other guys?"

This is your big chance to find an amazing guy, but finding someone great, someone perfect for you, is a *process*. It's possible you've felt an amazing bond with a guy before, and thought of him as "the one." But where did it get you? Ah yes, back to square one.

It's time to try something different for a change. You're going to play the field, meet men with different likes and different personalities. Even if you think a guy won't be a perfect fit, I want you to go out on a date with him. Similarly, if you go on a date with a guy who sweeps you off your feet, *don't just cancel all your other dates for the week*. Resist the urge to fall for a guy until you've dated him for a few months. And while you're dating him, I want you dating **other** men as well!

"Gregg, it seems almost rude to be dating more than one guy. What if I hurt someone's feelings?"

First off, if you think you're the only woman this guy is seeing, then you're sorely mistaken. Guys date more than one woman at the same time *all* the time. They're playing the field, testing out the waters, seeing who they like and don't like. Your first date with a guy may be the fourth first date he's been on that *week*. Dating is all about having options. The person who has more options is going to be more likely to find a person they really like. Simple as that.

The earlier you learn to play the field and date multiple partners, the better!

Now, it's important not to throw it in a man's face that you're "seeing other people on the side."

But you can show you're doing this in subtle ways. The first way to do it is to make sure you maintain an *active* profile on all of the dating sites you're using. This means adding new photos of yourself, rewriting your profile page from time to time and commenting on any forums or message boards.

Trust me, guys who find you on dating sites will often look at your profile again after the date. If they enjoyed the date at all, and they find you attractive, they'll visit your profile again. And when they do, guess what? They'll see *new* pictures and comments written after your date with them. This indicates you're still looking. When they realize their charm wasn't enough, they'll be left with the questions of "what could I have done better?" and "does she like me?" That's **exactly** where you want to be!

The same thing goes for the world of offline dating. Let's say you meet a guy at a MeetUp group. Great! Tell him you really enjoy these MeetUps and you hope to see him again, but then *don't* show up at the next one. Instead, head to another MeetUp and talk to people there! You can still go back the next week and talk to the guy (who is now very interested in seeing you again because you're much more mysterious to him) and continue the conversation where it left off.

A woman's edge is her mystery

By now you're probably getting a feel for where I'm going. Mystery, it seems, is one of the most effective ways of capturing a man's attention. It's for this reason that I recommend you avoid writing a novel about yourself on any of your dating profiles. Same goes for telling your date everything about you the first time you go out to dinner.

Let's say, for instance, you've traveled to Europe a few times. You're probably very proud of that trip and you'd like your date to know it. So you'll go out of your way to steer the conversation in that direction. "Oh, this Italian food isn't nearly as good as the real deal. Have you ever been to Europe?"

I get it - we all want to show off our best side during the first few dates with a person. And we're all looking for conversation starters when nerves are high and we're all dreading the silence between conversations. The trick here is to relax, and focus on a *detail* of something impressive you did, rather than the whole picture.

In the quote above, the woman is trying to steer the conversation toward her travels in Europe. She probably went to lots of places there and wants to show it off. Instead, she could have focused on one place, like Rome. That way, three dates from now, she can suddenly tell her date a story about when she was in Munich, Germany. "You were in Germany, too?" "Yes, I absolutely loved it!" And when he says, "wow, where *else* have you been," throw him a curve ball: "here and there. I traveled a lot in my 20's. How about you?"

It's all about measuring the pace of what you tell a person. Imagine how powerful it would be if you knew a man for over a year and during a conversation, he relates how he used to snowboard in the Alps. "What the heck?! How did I not *know* this about you?" Suddenly you're left wondering what *else* this person has done. This adds another layer of attraction and makes this person seem much more valuable.

Mystery is also about sex

Mystery and attraction go hand-in-hand. A woman who effectively shows off her features without being too provocative earns points in a man's eyes because he knows he hasn't seen all of you. The more you show off, the less mystery you have available to you, and the less attracted he is to you.

Women today are living on both Venus and Mars. When she's on Venus, she understands the value of her mystery, and how powerful attraction can be when she withholds sex. It adds to the mystery of her and it makes him want her more.

At the same time, women also live on Mars. She's free to have sex with any partner she wants, at any time she wants. Sounds great, right? It's the best of both worlds!

Here's the problem: you can't have both worlds. You can't pretend to have the same mystery and attraction of a woman from Venus when you're hanging out on Martian soil. If you give up sex freely to a man on the first date, you're basically telegraphing to him: "Hey, I'm just like you. If there's an opportunity for sex, I'll take it!"

In a nutshell, you'll be giving the guy what he *thinks* he wants, when in reality you're completely destroying any hope of a relationship. Plenty of guys will accept the offer of sex after a first date. Just don't expect these guys to make you breakfast the next morning. They'll be long gone, and in their eyes, you'll be a good time, and nothing more.

I have one small caveat to add. I said you can't live on both Venus and Mars, but this doesn't mean you can't *vacation* on one of them. While you're dating, if you want a relaxed, no-strings-attached sexual relationship, then by all means, go for it! Create a profile on Tinder or AshleyMadison.com and find a guy who you enjoy spending that kind of time with.

Just remember: you **cannot** date that guy in the same way you're dating men with relationship potential. You can get some on the side, but don't be confused by what that relationship is worth. When sex is freely given, you can't expect the relationship to be worth anything other than diddly squat.

Embracing Your Attraction and Setting the Pace of the Relationship

Women set the pace of the relationship. It doesn't matter how much control a man feels when he pays for your dinner and picks you up and buys you lovely things. You're the one who sets the pace. You're the one who holds the cards.

I discuss tactics like this in my dating confidence courses and many of my other dating eBooks. I invite you to check those out for even *more* detail on what I'm about to tell you. For now, I'm going to go over all of the essential concepts you need to lead the relationship in a direction of your choosing.

He pursues you, not the other way around. Ladies, you must make it appear that the man has control, and that means letting *him* be the one to call you and ask you out. Not only should a man make the first move, he should also be the one to call after a date.

The reasoning for this is simple. Men desire women who aren't easy to get. If you call him, you show your hand *way* too soon. Now he knows you like him. This, in turn, gives a subtle hint to him that he already has you, which in turn diminishes your attractiveness.

Never be the last person to text or send a message. Have you ever sent a text message or messaged a guy on some dating site and sat there waiting for a response? Awful feeling, right? Wouldn't it be great if that never happened again?

Great, because it never will! In my dating courses I teach that the person who texts or writes back last loses the attraction game. If you're having a conversation with a guy in a text or message format, you should never be the one sending the last response.

Here's a text example:

John: *Hi Carole, just wanted to confirm tonight. Picking you up at 8 right?*

You: *Yup! Sounds perfect John* ☺

John: *Great, looking forward to it!*

In this example, you could have responded with something like "me too!" or some other nonsense, but it would defy the rule above. In most cases you can manage it to where his response is the final word in a conversation. What he *wants* is for you to write him back and confirm his excitement. But you won't give it to him. Why? Because it takes away from your mystery. He'll feel slightly jittery because you didn't write back and his brain will go into overdrive wondering whether you're excited or not. That's right where you want him!

Keep how you feel about him under wraps. I mentioned earlier it's okay to say you had a good time, and you like the guy. That's okay and it's nice to confirm the guy is doing well so far. What I don't want you to do is get so caught up with him that you're practically swooning whenever he comes by.

Keep your emotions to yourself, for a **good**, **long** while. If he knows you like him, it gives him *real* power in the relationship, which isn't where you want him. You want him wondering, you want him to think you're still not sold on him.

Be the one to end the date/get off the phone. There's a slightly awkward moment near the end of the date when neither one of you are sure whether to be the one to get up first and end it. I'm telling you you should *always* be the one to do so. In most cases you don't need an excuse. You can just grab your purse and he'll get the hint. If you think you need an excuse just look at your watch, mention how fast time went by, and say you need to head home.

Same goes for phone conversations. You want to be the one to end it. Even if you have to lie, find an excuse, and say you have to go. Again, this is important because you're subtly controlling the conversation and ending it on *your* terms. If you wait for him to say he has to go then he has won the attraction game. Then you'll be the one wondering what it was he had to do that was so important that he had to get off the phone with you.

Sometimes, all the mystery and attraction
in the world won't be enough.

There will come a time when *none* of this works. Either a guy never called you back, or you get the impression that the date isn't working out. It isn't a matter of *if* it happens, it's a matter of *when*. Below we'll discuss what you need to know about rejection, and why you should **never** react to it.

He Loves Me, He Loves Me Not
Here it is, in all of its glory, the Golden Rule of Dating: **Never Dissect, Always Accept.**

Let me explain. You ladies go absolutely bonkers trying to figure out why a guy never called you back.

You've been rejected, and you want to understand why. It feels like a personal attack. If you can't figure it out, you'll just keep making the same mistake again and again. You need to figure it out. You need to, you need to!

If you date in this manner, you're going to have a rough few months. You may give up entirely, or worse, settle for a guy who isn't all that great but doesn't reject you right off the bat.

You must stop dissecting your every move to try to figure out where "you" went wrong. That's because it may not even be about you at all. Men all want different things. If you try to find things to change about yourself, you'll just become less authentic, which in turn means you're attracting the wrong guys for you.

Own yourself. Own every inch of you, own every personality trait. Stop dissecting what could have gone wrong, and learn to accept yourself and the decision of that particular guy.

I don't ever want you to write me saying how you were devastated because so-and-so didn't call you and now you want to call him to ask him why. This is the biggest dating no-no in the book! No matter how desperate you are to figure it out, you *must* accept that he decided against another date and move on!

Whether it was the fact that he considered you overweight, or he thought you were boring, or he thought you looked like his ex-wife, **none** of it matters and stressing over it will slowly wear down your confidence. Remember, your confidence is like a shield protecting you against crappy guys. If you lose it, you lose any hope of making your *own* choices and finding a guy who's right for **you**.

Chapter 4 Close Up

We're closing up Chapter 4, and with it, the book!
What we learned:

- Men are attracted to women who have their own life and live their life in a confident manner. This can manifest in many ways. It could be the job she has, the hobbies she loves, and the people in her life, just to name a few.

- Dating multiple partners at the same time may take some getting used to, but it's the absolute **best** thing you can do while you're dating. Get out there and date as many guys as you can. You can never have too many options!

- In the game of attraction, mystery is your biggest asset. Never give away everything about you. When you suddenly surprise him with either a hobby you're into or a place you've been after a month or more into the relationship, his interest in you will go through the roof.

- You **must** set the pace of the relationship. Let a man think he has control over it. But at the end of the day, you're the one who decides how fast or slow it moves.

- Never dissect, always accept. Stay true to yourself, accept a man's decision for not calling you, and don't dwell on guys who turn you down.

About the Author

Gregg feels coaching has chosen him. He grew up just as many others – in a dysfunctional, but loving family. After going through twelve years of his own failed relationships, he decided to try and decode dating for men *and* women. That elusive older couple sitting in the park holding hands gave him hope!

Gregg began his journey into understanding the mistakes we make in dating and how to fix them by interviewing thousands of people – happy couples, unhappy couples, singles looking for 'the one' and everyone in between. He reviewed his own dating experiences and combined all of this information into his series of dating advice books for men and women.

Outside of his work as one of Boston's top dating coaches, Gregg is involved in many things, including Wounded Warriors, animal shelters and construction. If you want to really tug at his heartstrings, come a'yodeling with a warm chocolate chip cookie in one hand and a rescue kitty in the other!

Gregg also believes in balancing his life and does so through high-energy activities like working out, jet-skiing, surfing and sailing. These activities, combined with more calming pursuits which include meditation, reading and hanging out near palm trees provide him with a full, balanced life.

Gregg's greatest thrill, however, probably comes from his work in helping women better understand men. His collection of dating advice books for women is designed to help women not only understand men better, but to understand themselves better. Gregg enjoys interacting with his readers through email and his coaching services and loves hearing about how women are starting to win their men back!

MORE BOOKS

Mr He - was - not what I
thought - he - was.

- Never justify a guy's
behaviour

- Having a social life boosts your confidence
- You need to feel good to look good
- wear what makes you Hot
- go for a makeover.

* Ask help from the younger generation for a fresh look.

* Confidence comes when you define your own true life. Don't let a man or anyone define your own life. You'll lose your freedom w—

Don't be complacent in your singleness after widowhood + divorce

— confidence is like a beacon / lighthouse for the world to see.

— If you want to find + keep a life partner never loose value of yourself

book page 11-12

— If you want change in your f. Start Now for transformation to happen immediately. It is always a matter How you w— do it Not when

Made in the USA
Middletown, DE
04 January 2019